TRANSITIONS

POEMS

TRANSITIONS

POEMS

H. C. Kim

The Hermit Kingdom Press
Cheltenham   Seoul   Bangalore   Cebu

TRANSITIONS: POEMS

ISBN: 0-9723864-6-7

Mailing Address:
The Hermit Kingdom Press
Suite 407
3741 Walnut Street
Philadelphia, PA 19104
USA

http://www.TheHermitKingdomPress.com

In celebration of their transitions in life, I dedicate this volume to my church friends who graduated from Cambridge University this year:

Bizzy Cole (history, Sidney Sussex College)
Heather Jones (law, St. Catharine's College)
Rachel Saunders (English, Trinity Hall)

PREFACE

Poems in this volume represent writing over 3 years, mostly in Cambridge, United Kingdom, but also in Bangalore, India. As many poets do, I take much poetic freedom to express and capture the essence of human experiences. We are all different as individuals but share commonness of being humans. I hope that I have succeeded in capturing something beautiful in our shared experiences as members of the human race. May we all make this world a better place in our stations in life.

H. C. Kim
Jesus College
Cambridge
July 4, 2004
American Independence Day

"Visions *of* as well as for the church were known at the time of Christian origins. The dreamers of dreams in Israel saw the people as a threatened flock, and Jerusalem as a mourning and rejoicing mother and bride (1 En. 89-91; 2 Esd. 9-10); and the Christians followed them with visions of the church and the holy city as a mother and bride, an aged yet joyful woman and a tower (Rev. 12.1-6, 19.7-8, 12.2; Hermas, *Vis.* i-iii)."

Professor William Horbury of Cambridge University

CONTENTS

Contents

Transitions

"A Friendly Bee"

A friendly bee
Flies
Gliding across the sky
So blue

Buzzing around
In perfect circles
Approaching beautiful flowers
Gracefully

Like a glider
Let loose from a cliff
Only to descend
Like a bird

Making the whole world hers
She flies and flies
In a beautiful bed of roses
Passionate red

The sun shining
Brightly above
In warm adoration
As the adorable bee comes

In the vast field
Extending into the great distant
Becomes her domain
For frolic and happiness

"Almost There"

The football flies high
In the sky blue
Spring
Penetrating the thin air

The football ascends
Like a rocket fired from below
Thrusting forward
In a powerful climb

Lingering in the vastness
Under the deep blue gaze
Even covering the bright sunshine
It flies and flies

Then the football descends
Dropping down towards the ground
Like an apple falling
Gravity exerting its pull

I run and run
Towards the beautiful
Gift from the sky
Not wanting to drop her

Miss her
I run and run
Hoping to catch her
As she flies free and unfettered

I jump and extend my arms
As she continues her run

I can feel no ground below me
And I am almost there

"The Clock Tower"

The clock tower reaches into the skies
Like the positive spirit
That has driven mighty peoples
Into distant lands

Its beautiful stature
Finely shaped and managed
Stands with an austere presence
Standing tall in the city

Every detail
Shows intricate care
Love poured on her
People protecting her like they would
    themselves

She watches over the city
Like a patroness
Who loves her people
Her city more than herself

Ever the presence
An identity maker
Which symbolizes us all
She is goodness embodied

She imprints her image
On all who behold her
As if she holds magical powers
She stands tall and beautiful

Distant she is

Perhaps I can approach her
And feel a part of her being
Metaphysically and existentially linked

"Happiness"

What is happiness but a state of being?
Can it be generated?
Can it be created?

What makes one happy?
Can everyone find it?
Can anyone find it?

Happiness is a state of being
A locality
If you stumble into it
Stay in it

Hold onto happiness
Like there is no tomorrow
As if nothing else matters
Can you find it again?

Time flies
People change
Settings alter themselves
And you remain

To find happiness
To possess it
Does anything else matter?
To remain happy

"It Is Christmas Again"

It is Christmas again
Time just seems to fly
It seems like yesterday
That I celebrated the last Christmas

I remember what I hoped for
As if I were in a déjà vu repeat
Hope upon hope
Desire after desire

Life flows
Quickly like a rushing stream
From on high to the pond below
Carrying its residue with it

Life changes
New born came into the world
My best friend had his love bundle
She's my goddaughter

I remember their first date
It seems ages ago
Now they have formed a loving family
Children to carry on their name and being

I sit amazed at the changes in life
Time flies and Christmas marks each year
There is a pretty tree nearby
With Christmas bright-lights shining

It is Christmas again

I wonder how many of my friends are
happy
Truly happy to be where they are
Do they feel fulfilled?

Time flies
New children will be born
I only wish all my friends could be happy
I guess they would know

"Like Memory"

I wonder what she is thinking
Now in her own space and time
In her little world
Her comfort zone

Far removed from the world here
All that seemed real
Now must appear like mere memory
Past ephemeral reality

Who is she in this world?
What does she feel?
What does she want?
What is she willing to sacrifice?

I wonder about the path ahead
Her path ahead
That links her past
To her present

I think about my present
And our space in time
In this confused world
That we belong to

Present, past, and future
Seem to merge
In a parallel reality
She in her comfort zone and me in mine?

"New Life"

New Life
That's what they want to make
New life for whom?
For what?

Can happiness come for them?
Are they truly happy now?
Can they forge a new life?
With hope and happiness

More power to them
If they can
They deserve to be happy
I would not wish anything else

New life
Forever
As far as eternity on earth goes
The whole life

New life
Formed to give happiness
To contribute to the world
To continue life

In an old world
Which gets older every year
New life is made together
United in being

Bringing freshness
And happiness

To the already existent mess
Chaos that is the world

"Running"

She runs and runs
Away from what
I cannot tell

She is a fleeting beautiful
With a friendly smile
That transcends reality

In her eyes
Is a glitter that shines
Brighter than the stars of the sky

She runs and runs
Like she is running away
From something she desires

She looks content
In her little world
Beautifully arranged by her

But there is something missing
What could it be?
What will make her complete?

She runs and runs
Even when she walks
Even when she stands

I want to run with her
To stop her from running
Just to hold her

To say that all will be okay
She doesn't have to run
If she doesn't want to

If she wants to
I will run with her
As long as we are together also in spirit

"She Reads On"

She sat there
Absorbed in her book
Looking into it

But her thoughts
Seemed to wander
Even as her eyes fixed on the book

I cast a quick glance
Hoping that she wouldn't notice
Even though I was not in the wrong

She read and read on
As I tried to comprehend her
Trying to figure out how I might turn her
    pages

Her mobile phone sat there
Sticking out among the surrounding
    books
In its blank mystery

She read on and on
As I tried to understand
What was before me

"Smile"

She stood in silence
In her welcoming outfit
With a fleeting smile on her gentle face

She smiled
In mysterious complexity
Couching her thoughts

I smiled
Not knowing quite what to say
And just smiled

"The Answer"

Through her eyes
I can see
I can see something

Her blue eyes
Beautifully shield
Her inner thoughts

Her practiced smile
Charming and sweet
Shows her gentle disposition

Her manners
Slow and deliberate
Exhibit her self-control

But I can see
A spark of fire
In her eyes

A kind of restless longing
For something
Searching for wholeness

What is she searching for?
What does she want to find?
What does she desire?

I look into her eyes
Wanting to find the answers
The blueness of her eyes

It is so blue and so vast
Like the deep blue sea
Full of life and activity

I see the spark grow
Her eyes becoming brighter and brighter
As I search for the answer

"Two Snowballs"

It's like two snowballs flying in the air
They fly from one origin to another
With a purpose
Their origin and destination are
    determined

In a snowball fight
Snowballs fly against each other
Origins are opposed
Destinations are contrary targets

Father and son
Throwing snowballs at a tree
Two snowballs fly from the same origin
To hit the same target

Snowballs
Made of the same matter
With similar capabilities
Can be cast in one direction or the other

That's like life
There are many snowballs
That can go in one direction or the other
Origin and destination can determine
    outcome

Two snowballs come against each other
Or they can glide together through the
    skies
Who will determine the outcome?
Who will make the origin matter?

"Winter Wonderland"

Of memories past
And possibilities of the future
I limp
Not being aware

What is out there
What pain there was
What blessings there will be
I am oblivious

Slowly limping
Across the old winter streets
I can feel the cold breeze
Climbing up my leg

The warmth of my Christmas sweater
Comforts me
As I amble across
The familiar streets

Less friendly faces
Less people
It seems
It is the Christmas vacation

I move
Always forward
Forgetful of past incursions
Unaware of future potential

I am in the present
In the coldness of it

Engulfed in the freshness
Of winter wonderland

"A Life Shared"

When I think of you
I think of a life shared
Passions as well as the mundane
Life as well as suffering

Holding your hand tightly
As I confess my unbridled love to you
Even in times when sorrow overtakes you
Your face filled with tears

I would hold your hands tight
And would not let you go
I will be there to shield you
To protect and uphold you

I would be your greatest champion
Most eager lover
A faithful husband and a supportive friend
And I would take your fantasies to the
       next level

Together, we will make the world move
United, we will add joy to the lives of many
For our joy would overflow and there will
       be more to share
You will smile not from form but because
       you can't contain yourself

You and I will be two lovers of which
       fairytales are made
We will create with boundless creativity
Energy generated in powerful combustion

As our union realigns the stars of heaven

A few experience the union of souls meant
    to be united
Such is your soul and mine
Not a union of mere situation
But a destiny guided by purposeful fate

You and I will share
In the triumph of possibilities
And the human potential
It will be gratifying and meaningful

For we will fulfill every desire we have
And some which have not entered our
    minds before
We will find ecstasy in every inch of each
    other's soul
And emotional gratification in the
    pleasures beyond the physical

We will be a team
Two bodies in one
Working together to bring meaning to
    others
A team designed in heaven

All you have to do is say, "Yes"
I do
I do choose to be happy beyond my
    imagination
I choose to be with you the rest of my life

You, I have already decided
The moment I first saw you

That you are the one for me
That my life would be complete with your
    hand in mine

"Cruel Fate"

It is a cruel fate
That we are still kept apart
As you and I are meant to be together
Sharing future dreams together

Why are you out there
Wherever you are
Away from me
And my touch?

Why am I here
Missing you
Longing for your face
To smell you next to me

It is a cruel fate
That I do not yet hold your hand
Beautifully fashioned with God's attention
    to detail
That your hand is not placed interwoven
    in mine

You are there so far away
As if there are several universes between
    us
Like stars at the opposite ends of the
    world
But we should be together two peas in a
    pod

Where are you?
I hear your soul calling out for me

And my soul searching for you
Like the undead of ancient myths who
    seek fulfillment

"Flowing"

Her hair flowed
Like the effervescence of Iguazu Falls
Filled with might
Characterized by an emphatic presence

Her face radiated
Like a mother seeing her babe for the first
    time
A child having his favorite lollypop
An adult looking wishfully at a Harley-
    Davidson

Her arms gently moved
Like regal trees of Cambridgeshire
Making their presence known
With benevolence

Her beautiful legs moved
Like time advancing inevitably
Like history being made
As the pyramids of Egypt shine brightly

I stood there
Like one marveling before an imaginary
    spaceship
One who has seen the collapse of the
    Empire State Building
Like Moses who had just seen God

"I Smile"

I smile because I see her in my mind
I laugh because I think of the joy I can
    share with her
She gives me hope that makes me feel
    alive
She is my most treasured memory

I wish every time that it would be her
Whom I would hold and caress
To adore and shower my affections upon
To hold in my arms to show her she is
    loved

She is to me woman I love
Above all else that she is
My soul reaches out to her
As I connect with her without much
    background knowledge

Call me lazy
For not investigating her friends and
    relatives
Call me stupid
For allowing my heart to go out to her in
    seeming ignorance

But I know this to be true
That I adore her because I know her
Beyond formalities and mere form
Beyond who she knows and what she has
    accomplished

I love the way her smile incapacitates me
I see in her eyes a heart shining of virtue
    and goodness
I feel myself weak in her presence and
    proximity
I am intoxicated by her sweet aroma

She is to me like the morning sunshine
Brightly shining and ushering in a new
    day filled with hope
I can only smile as I see her in my mind's
    eye
I can actually laugh with a joy that
    overflows

She and I would create happiness
A whole new world of experience
Filled with hopes and dreams
Doing good where we can

Together
We will be
As 2-in-1
Drawn by love

And our love would last
As we find joy in the fulfillment of our
    souls
Meeting of two meant to be
Cosmic order aligned as it should be

I want her by my side
Not because of what she knows
Who she knows
What she has experienced

I want her
Because I desire her
She as I first saw her
She as who she is to me

"I Want To Walk Right Up To You"

I want to walk right up to you
Look into your eyes
And utter the words
"I love you."

But I dare not
Not because I fear what you will think of
      me
Even what you will say to me
But I don't know if you could manage

I know how I feel
And although we have not talked much
I feel I know you
I know all that I need to know to love you

We have talked from here to there
A few sporadic moments of conversation
Yet deeply meaningful
Memorable

So I am torn
Between my very selfish desire to have you
To hold you in my arms
Embrace you with a passion that you
      deserve

To kiss you gently on your lips
Your cheeks
Your forehead
Your hair

To taste the very essence of who you are
And be together in one
As our souls unite in common destiny
I want you above and over all else

Yet I do not feel you would be able to
    handle
The flood of passion
Ready to hear my immense affection for
    you
For you probably think that you still know
    me not

It is a consideration for you
And your misguided need for space
I await in stupid hesitation
Although I know I will be happy the rest of
    my life with you

Should I be selfish and assert myself
To convince you to embrace what you
    know deep in your heart
But haven't managed to accept
Perhaps you care about your place in
    society

If it weren't your sense of well-being
That concerned me
I would go forward to win you
And the prize will be me for you

Yet, we remain unfulfilled
And you relegated to a place of mediocre
    contentment
Comfortable yet lacking rapture

Which our union would provide

"Life of π"

Life of π
Like life of pie
Like life of pile
Like life of mile
Like life of tile
Like life of aisle
Like life of isle
Like life of ire
Like life of tire
Like life of fire
Like life of dire
Like life of squire
Like life of quagmire
Like life of choir
Like life of repertoire
Like life of martyr
Like life of peuter
Like life of banter
Like life of cantor
Like life of tenor
Like life of honor
Like life of pun-er
Like life of punter
Like life of partner
Like life of fencer
Like life of dancer
Like life of bouncer
Like life of trouncer
Like life of trout
Like life of crowd
Like life of proud
Like life of wound

Like life of pound
Like life of bound
Like life of found
Like life of ground
Like life of frown
Like life of hound
Like life of ounce
Like life of once
Like life of hence

"One Page"

Curtains overlap
Like two pages in a book
Filled with suspense and anticipation
One page transforming the next

A lot can happen in one page
People can die
People can be saved
World can come to an end

From this page to that
A space of one page
Transformative
World-shaking

It is that one second
Where two exchange a look
A vow of everlasting love is made
A tie stronger than all the useless words
    uttered

One page of a book
One look shared
How the world can be shaken
How lives can be changed

She is the one page
That essential one page
That changes the whole book
Who moves the world underneath me

"Pen Is Turning And Turning"

Pen is turning and turning
Reflecting the summer light
With each artificial turn

Light cascades down
The corridors of Big Medium Pen
As residue of used ink lingers in the tube

Like capturing the vast skies
With all its spotted clouds
Myriad of blueness

Endless extension of hope
Stretching far, far beyond
Into the invisible reality

Defying its purpose
Merely as a writing instrument
The pen shines gloriously in the spotlight

Like a beautiful prism
A useful flashlight
The transparent pen glares white light

As the pen rolls and rolls between the
    fingers
Even its blue tip radiates flashes of bright
    light
As the pen transforms itself

Into a lightning rod
One summer day

Shining and shining

"Questions For You"

Do you think me a coward
For longing you but not
Approaching you?

Do you think me cruel
For withholding my deep affections
From you as I so wish otherwise?

Do you think me stupid
For letting time fly by
Without you close to my heart?

Do you think me odd
To long for you moment after moment
But only from afar?

Do you think me crazy
For not stopping to hold the moment
The only sane thing in this city?

Do you think me weak
For letting you pass me by
When you alone give me strength?

"The Dream"

Do you know that I dreamed
The day before yesterday
A dream of you?

There you were in my arms
As I held your soft back
With my left arm

As I gently bushed strands of hair from
    your face
My right hand touching your cheeks
As I looked deeply into your eyes

In a dream
In my deep sleep
I spoke to you in poetry

"The winds of spring are here
Carrying the winds of fall
As the summer winds heat up."

Before I could say another word
Your beautiful eyes took a look of reproach
And you spoke to me

In uncharacteristic bluntness
Yet in forthright
Honesty

There in my arms
You asked,
"When will the summer winds heat up?"

And I was stunned
By the cold honesty of your words
And I knew not what to say

And you took my hesitation as a sign
Of my lack of love for you
As I looked at your eyes filling with doubt

But I felt you in my arms
And knew that it would be okay
That there you were

Even while you were teasing me
With rebuke frolicking in your eyes,
    saying,
"I can report you."

Puzzled, I looked at you
Trying to understand the meaning of your
    tease
As you lay there in my arms

And I felt you and your wonderful
    presence
As I woke from my dream
My longing for you I still felt intensely

"Auto-Rickshaw"

Purring like a mad kitten in heat
With energetic vibration
Moving slowly
But always in motion

The auto-rickshaw purrs along
Down the main road in Bangalore
The constant vibration moves all inside
With constant rhythmic motion

The floor underneath moves
As buildings pass by in the opposite
        direction
Speed picking up
The vehicle shakes with gusto

The occasional gust of wind
Brushes my naked arm gently
I could even feel the little hairs caressed
The loose clothing flutters against my
        body

Somehow I feel not alone
But rather violated
Like being out in the open
For all to see

The auto-rickshaw speeds along
Without a door
No windows
It is meant to be a road show

How could I enjoy the ride
With the open air
And the freedom one could experience
When I feel the eyeballs around me?

It's like a secret pleasure
That is kept deep inside
With a stone face to cover the real emotion
The gush of effusion

Like under invisible sheets
And behind transparent doors
I rest
Being self-conscious

The auto-rickshaw moves slightly
From side to side
Making a squeaky sound
Perhaps the weight is not evenly
        distributed

I could swear that the woman on the
        street
Is gawking at the auto-rickshaw
And the pleasure that I derive
Shining through my forced stone
        expression

The inner ecstasy cannot be contained
Even despite the horrific odor
That seems to flood the auto-rickshaw
Everything recedes into the background

There is the auto-rickshaw and me
Very public and visible

But also very personal and private
I find a small circle of personal pleasure

Who would have imagined
So much happening inside such a visible
    but closed space?
My auto-rickshaw purrs along
And I along with it

"Bangalore's Calling"

I can hear the call of friendly voices in
    Bangalore
Wrapped in thousands of years of India's
    beautiful traditions
Yet advanced in all things important and
    modern
Technological center of the world
One can easily say
I can almost see the auto-rickshaw taxis
    swerving
Picking up friendly passengers
Motorcycles with traditionally clad wives
Holding fast to their gentle husbands
Young hurrying to the latest Bollywood
    films
Many of them will surely be leaders of
    tomorrow
Leading in technology and industry
Hopefully there will be great spiritual
    leaders among them as well
I can picture in my mind the friendly faces
    that I have seen
Familiar faces of encouragement and
    support
Beauty of India
Hope of India
Bangalore will not be forgotten
It is not easily forgettable
I can hear it calling me
Beckoning me to be back very soon
And share in its wonders
Partake of its friendship

Yet again

"Barking"

A dog barks
Another one responds
Soon
A chorus of barking dogs

Where are they all?
Don't they ever sleep?
Do these canines not need a glass of
    water?
All the noise without pause!

In the darkness of night
With no visible street lights
From the pitch dark room
I look out into the invisible

Darkness surrounds the yelping dogs
Orgy ridden noise so horrific
There must be some canine
Sadomasochistic acts unimaginable

In unknowable canvas called darkness
I lie awake painting
Feelings of fatigue in every inch of my
    body
Kept awake by unholy yelling of the beasts

Were this artwork displayed in
A museum of modern art
It would be a blank canvas
Colored pure black

Were this a film playing in theatres
It would play in the most high end art
    cinemas
Even a blind man would be able to see it
    and hear
The non-stop barking in darkness without
    a hint of light

Dogs are barking
And barking
Like non-stop techno music
It has its consistency in the midst of chaos

I lie half-awake
Wondering when all the barking will end
Soon I can't tell if I am hearing them
    actually barking
Or having a nightmare dream sequel to
    reality

"Construction"

I see the beams
Wooden beams
Holding up the concrete structure
Not yet complete
With workers dangling from the poles
Like monkeys from trees

They do things differently over here
I am told
Yes, it doesn't look anything like
Construction sites I have seen before in
    the USA
No hard hats
No signs of warning

I walk through the site
Forgetful of danger over my head
I don't think about the accidents that
    could befall
The story of how half a dozen died
In a construction site accident
I think it was in New York

No
I don't think about
How a brick could fall and hit me on the
    head
My unprotected head
I see hat-free heads all around me
But I haven't heard of a building
    construction accident in Bangalore

How do they build wooden beams so tall
and wide?
How is it so sturdy?
I marvel as I gaze at people working on the
building
But surely this building is being built to
completion
I can see it with my own eyes
Workers laboring away

You could see pride in the eyes
Their skin dark black from working in the
sun
Way too long
Their muscles drenched in sweat
Dust covering their body
They sure must be envisioning the final
product

What an experience
To walk through a construction site
Being built without a blueprint
Constructed by ones with no conventional
education
But they have the experience
They have built many buildings before

This building will surely be built
And it will be grandiose
Like all the other structures they have
built
Next year
I will see the final product
And think back about this walk through
the site

"Draught"

The roads are dry
Dust thick in the atmosphere
You can almost see it
Feel it

It is monsoon season
But the expected rain is missing
Where are the clouds
Bringing good news of water from heaven?

Heavenly gates should be opened
Treasure pouring down on earth
But water is lacking
Discontent brewing

The water truck passing by on the road
In Bangalore
Only reminds us
Draught has hit the land

All over the country
There is complaint of
Lack of water
So essential for everything

Where are the clouds
The sweet sound of thunder
Leaves rustling to harbinger the coming
    rain
Slight darkness before the rain fall?

It is dry

My throat feels scratchy
And I just feel like flapping my shirt
To bring some coolness to my body

Perhaps it could serve another purpose
A kind of my own private rain dance
People here need rain
I need rain

Should I stand up and do a two step?
Maybe that's more like a rain dance?
The sky shows no sign of monsoon
    showers
And there is just not enough water for a
    long shower

I sit down
With both hands on my cheeks
Both of my elbows on my knees
In a posture of defeat

"MG Road"

A trap for the Westerner
So declare travel guide books
In effect

A place for Indians
Who are westernized or want to be
In soothe

Cinemas playing movies in English
Name brands well known in the West sold
    here
Fast food joints like Kentucky Fried
    Chicken too

You see people busying themselves
Through the sidewalks
Too crowded to walk like a New Yorker

India's young will dominate the country
The local newspapers declare
And they all long to be Western

Savvy, shrewd, worldly
Is that what is meant?
Or bringing all that is seen as the failure
    of the West?

History is bound to repeat itself
So the historians tell us
It is like a sick joke

Will India repeat the errors of the West?

Will the society degenerate
With all that is evil with Capitalism?

Here on this road
You can see computer programmers
Who design programs for the whole world

There are India's new rich
Reapers of the benefits of the Internet
And they want to be a part of the West

MG Road
What it will be for the future of India?
How will India's young find answers for
    the future?

"Morning Run"

It's an ungodly hour
Early in the morning
When even the cows
So visible during daylight
Are in heavy slumber

Even the barking dogs have fallen silent
They must be in doggie dreamland
It's too early for anything
Except for sweet snoring
Even the poorest can lay claim to sleep at
    this hour

But here I am
In my sneakers
Trousers
Dress shirt
And a tie

Running like a mad businessman
Trying to meet a deadline
Obviously lacking regular exercise
Soon I find myself out of breath
But in my defense it is a wretchedly early
    morn

But I do my part
A member of the running team
Meant to build a group spirit
Perhaps
I run with my new found mates

They certainly look much more awake
    than I do
I think they must have done this for a long
    time
They are even smiling
While running with swift ease
Like gazelles talked about in the Bible

Through the small neighborhood in
    Kanahalli
Where a mixture of Tamil and Kannada
Are spoken as *lingua franca*
An area in Bangalore
We make our claim through our run

The sun has not yet risen
Even the sun is in slumber
But here we are
A bunch of young souls
With dreams brighter than the morning
    sunshine

"Mysore Silk Factory"

Rolls and rolls of silk
Hanging in the background
A makeshift wall paper
Colorful

Smooth to the touch
Local silk
Distinctive to the region
The salesperson insists

Soft
Slippery
Fluid
Flowing

White
Red
Pink
Beige

Silk diverse in texture
Content
Volume
Look

Meant to design clothing
Clinging to the body
In a perfect fit
Right match for one's particular form

Measurements to be taken
From head to toe

Chest, waist, hip
Arm and leg length

For the sweet flow of silk
All over one's bare figure
Aesthetics in fashion
Distinctive quality of local fashion

To slide swiftly in
With electrifying touch
Surprise even to one who is used to it
This is no ordinary silk

Measurements taken
Suit produced
Outcome splendid
All a day's work

One of a kind
It certainly is not
Mysore silk factories
Color the city's landscape

But the individual experience
Personal and particular
Of Mysore silk on one's body
Clothing form-fitted specially

Embraced in silky glory
New possessed as own
Splendor that is India's creativity
A product of Mysore silk factory

"Nilgris Market"

In the middle of the bustle
A friendly place
Smiling faces inside
And not just a landmark
For an auto-rickshaw taxi

People walking
Cows grazing
Dogs barking
Dust everywhere
It is Kanahalli

With the coziness of a small house
Filled with sons and granddaughters
This part of Bangalore
Is homey in its own way
Certainly very busy

Impersonal it might be however
Outside
Perhaps because of the bustle
But inside the market
Friendly smiles

An inquisitive look here
A wayward question there
A curiosity borne
Not of malice
No imposition

Strange it is
How a market could feel

Like a home away from home
What is it about the place?
One cannot help but wonder

Visibly present
Nilgris Market stands as a monument
Town's people take pride in it
It is a landmark for auto-rickshaw
Taxis

You could pick one up
Get dropped off here
They know where it is
It's an axis mundi
For this cozy place

If you are a foreigner
Sojourning here for a little while
You better remember
Where this cozy landmark is
Or you'll be lost in the shuffle

May have to walk your mile
And might not even find the place
For neighborhoods look all alike
In this big city of Bangalore
Perhaps because I am new here

But certainly not only a taxi marker
Nilgris Market rewards those who enter
With a warm atmosphere
Products that strangely comfort
And it is not merely the magic of shopping
    either

"The Cows"

A cow here
A cow there
Cows everywhere
Frolicking in freedom

People pass by on the street
And do not even throw a second look
It is perfectly normal
How strange it is for me

I have seen
A dog here
A dog there
Dogs everywhere before

But cows?
Doesn't everybody see that they are
Cows?
They are not house pets!

But like cats
They walk the streets
Looking into street trash bins for food
Gazing at the walking humans

I wonder if I could approach them
These cows in the streets
Let loose
Living carefree

Can I go and pet them?
Touch their noses and ears?

Rub their stomachs?
Run my fingers through their heads?

I look around and see
What appears abnormal for me
Is totally normal for everyone else
And I wonder

"With"

With the rising of the sun
Arise the spirits
Eager for a new day
Filled with possibilities

With the dawning of a new day
Dawns the awakening
Realizing what is needed
What lies ahead

With the crowding of cumulus clouds
Crowd students
Wishing to learn
To gain understanding

With the rising of the summer heat
Rises the teacher
In front of his pupils
Wanting to impart something valuable

With the advancing of time
Advance the pages in the New Testament
Read out loud
In the class room in Bangalore

With the arrival of the evening
Arrives the reflection
The day past
Events transpired

With the descending of the night
Descend my eyelids

Worn out from the day's instruction
As joyful as it was